The Good Cook's Book of
ITALIAN
COOKING
Mary Reynolds

O9-ABE-835

CONTENTS

NOTES

Standard spoon and cup measurements are used in all recipes.
All spoon and cup measures are level.

Fresh herbs are used unless otherwise stated. If unobtainable substitute a bouquet garni of the equivalent dried herbs, or use dried herbs instead but halve the quantities stated.

Use freshly ground black pepper where pepper is specified.

Ovens should be preheated to the specified temperature.

This edition published 1982
by Octopus Books Limited
59 Grosvenor Street
London W1

© Cathay Books 1981
ISBN 0 7064 1721 6

Printed in USA

INTRODUCTION

The best cooking in Italy is found in the home. Italian women take a special pleasure in shopping for the best quality ingredients and in cooking attractive meals for their families.

The main meal of the day is an important event, a social occasion when all the family gather around the table to exchange the news and gossip of the day and to share in the enjoyment of "mama's" cooking. A traditional Italian meal – although infinitely flexible – generally consists of a *minestra* (soup, pasta dish or risotto), followed by a course of meat, fish or poultry with one or two vegetables. Sometimes a salad is served after the main course. The meal ends with cheese and fresh fruit in season, and is rounded off with a small cup of strong expresso coffee. On special occasions a simple antipasto may be served before the *minestra* and a dessert before the fruit and cheese.

Generally speaking, hard and fast rules have no place in the Italian kitchen, so use the recipes in this book as guidelines, always testing, trying and adapting as you go along.

Italian Regional Cooking

Until 1861, Italy was a collection of independent states, each with its own laws, customs and traditions. Today, as you travel from one area to another, you will notice regional differences between the landscape, people, dialects and foods.

There is a particularly marked difference between northern and southern Italy: regions in the north tend to be more industrial and prosperous than those in the poorer south and the northern soil tends to be more fertile. The differences as far as cooking is concerned are that the traditional northern pasta is the flat variety, freshly made with eggs; the fat used for cooking is generally butter. In the south, tubular varieties of pasta are more common and olive oil is used for cooking. Flavors are much stronger in the south because of the extensive use of herbs and spices, particularly in sauces.

Well-known pasta dishes of the northern province of Liguria include ravioli and minestrone soup. The rice-growing area in the Po Valley, just behind Venice, provides abundant supplies of arboreo rice. This especially absorbent medium-grained rice is available occasionally in speciality food stores and is the basis for risottos. Many delicious, creamy risotto recipes have evolved; risotto Milanese from Lombardy is one of the best known.

Two of the most famous products of the north are Parmesan cheese and prosciutto ham, both from Parma. Parmesan cheese is at its best after 2 years of drying and maturing, and gets stronger the older it becomes. The whey from the cheese is fed to the Parma pigs and, combined with the careful salting and drying processes on the hillsides, results in the delicately flavored ham.

Italy is surrounded on three sides by sea and locally caught fish are a dominant feature of most regional cuisines. Venice is particularly noted for its red and grey mullet, squid, scampi and mussels. In the north, deep sea fish are supplemented by excellent freshwater fish from the Lakes of Lombardy – especially eels. The southern coast and the islands of Sicily and Sardinia are dotted with fishing villages. Here, tuna, sardines, swordfish and a variety of shellfish are caught and used locally in pasta dishes, sauces, soups, stews and salads.

Abundant local supplies of tomatoes, garlic, herbs and anchovies in the southern regions give dishes their characteristic aromatic quality. Naples, the culinary center of the south, claims the invention of the pizza and ice cream as we know it today. Pizzas are baked in open-brick

Milan
Turin
Piedmont
Genoa
Bologna
Venice
LIGURIAN SEA
Florence
Tuscany
Corsica
ADRIATIC SEA
Rome
Bari
Naples
Sardinia
Calabria
Palermo
Sicily
MEDITERRANEAN SEA

ovens of pizzerias and bakeries, and most often eaten as
snacks. Mozzarella, the cheese used for pizza topping, has
been made for centuries in the surrounding countryside of
Campania. It is an ideal "melting" cheese and lends itself
to all types of pizzas and cooked dishes. The equally
famous Italian ices are made in mouth-watering flavors
and, like the pizza, have spread all over Italy and around
the world.

Italy is the world's largest wine producer and almost
every region makes its contribution to the great vareity of
exported table wines. Piemonte is the home of Barolo, a
fine red to serve with roast meat and game, and the modest
but flavorsome Barbera, an ideal wine to drink with robust
pasta dishes and pizzas. Veneto provides two popular
wines: the dry, red Valpolicella and Soave – a medium
white wine. From Tuscany comes the deservedly famous
Chianti Classico, the perfect accompaniment to roasts,
broiled meat and game. Other Italian wines worth trying
are Orvieto, Verdicchio, Frascati and Lambrusco.

7

Specialist Italian Ingredients

Delicatessens and supermarkets sell a wide variety of Italian ingredients.

CHEESES

Parmesan: Unique cheese, grated and added to sauces, pasta, rice and other dishes to give an incomparable flavor. Buy it in chunks and grind it at home. Bottles of pre-grated Parmesan cannot compare with freshly grated.

Mozzarella: A white cheese, used extensively in cooking for its melting properties, especially as a topping for pizzas. It is sold in packages but, when bought fresh, is moist and dripping with whey. Bel Paese can be used as a substitute.

Ricotta: A soft, white cheese, made from whey. Must be eaten absolutely fresh. Used in stuffings and sweet fillings.

Gorgonzola: The famous Italian blue-veined table cheese. When ripe, it should be mild and soft.

Other Italian cheeses to look for are Bel Paese, Romano, Fontina, Provolone and Caciocavallo.

CURED MEATS AND SAUSAGES

Prosciutto: Delicately cured ham, eaten smoked and wafer thin. The best comes from Parma or San Daniele. No real substitute, but for cooked dishes use cooked ham.

Salami: Long dry-cured sausages of lean ground meat with pork fat and spices. There are various types, of which Salami Milano is considered the best. Serve sliced in mixed antipasti, chopped in stuffings.

Mortadella: Large smooth-textured cooked pork sausage laced with pork fat and spices. Serve sliced for antipasti, chopped in stuffings.

Cotechino: Lightly cured pork sausage, weighing from 1 to 2 lb. First it is boiled, then thickly sliced and served with lentils or beans, or cold with salad.

Luganega: Long, thin coiled sausage of mild, coarsely ground pork. Also called *Salsiccia*. Fry, broil or boil and serve hot with lentils or potatoes. Any fresh sausage with a high meat content can be used as a substitute.

HERBS

Herbs are an essential flavoring in many Italian dishes. Fresh herbs are normally used in Italy. It is well worth growing the herbs you cannot buy in pots on the window sill or in the garden. Use dried herbs when fresh are unavailable, but replace dried herbs regularly to avoid staleness. The following herbs are used most commonly in Italian cooking.

Basil: The incomparable herb for tomato dishes. Also popular in salads, sauces and soups.

Bay Leaves: As a flavoring for casseroles, stews, soups and roasts.

Oregano: An ingredient used in many dishes, especially pizzas, casseroles and sauces.

Parsley: The universal herb for flavoring Italian dishes. Italian parsley is the flat-leaved variety so use this when available.

Rosemary: Strongly-flavored herb, used mainly for roast lamb or pork. Also used in chicken and fish dishes.

Sage: Especially for flavoring veal and chicken dishes cooked in wine.

PANTRY INGREDIENTS

The following non-perishable ingredients are frequently used in Italian dishes and it is useful to keep a stock of them in your pantry.

Pasta: Available in an immense variety of shapes and used in many different ways: both the shaped pastas of the south (macaroni, spaghetti, zita, bucatini, rigatoni, etc) and the lighter, flat egg pastas of the north (tagliatelle, fettucine, lasagne, etc). Keep a variety of different kinds of pasta on hand – including a few of the less usual shapes and small varieties for soups.

Rice: Italian arboreo rice is thick and short and absorbs more liquid than other types of rice. It is used to make creamy risotto. Occasionally available in speciality food stores.

Beans: Dried beans and lentils, canned white cannellini and red kidney beans are used for soups, salads and other dishes.

Pepper and Salt: Italians always use freshly ground black peppercorns from a pepper mill and, when possible, coarse sea salt.

Wine Vinegar: Essential for salad dressings and used in many other recipes.

Olive and Vegetable Oils: The distinctive flavor of good olive oil is needed for salad dressings and for cooking because olive oil gives the dish a special character. Otherwise ground nut or sunflower oils are suitable.

Anchovy Fillets in oil: For adding zest to sauces, pizzas and antipasti dishes.

Capers: Small capers add authenticity to many sauces, fish dishes and garnishes.

Olives: Keep small bottles of green, ripe and stuffed olives on hand, but buy fresh loose olives when possible.

Canned Tomatoes: Italian plum, crushed and whole peeled tomatoes have an excellent flavor and are time-saving and convenient to use for sauces and casseroles.

Tomato Paste: Small amounts are invaluable for strengthening the flavor and color of dishes in which fresh or canned tomatoes are used.

Fortified Wines: Dry white Vermouth can be used in recipes calling for dry white wine and herbs. Medium Marsala adds a richness to veal, poultry and ham dishes.

SAUCES

Salsa di Fegatini
Chicken Liver Sauce

4 tablespoons butter
1 small onion, chopped
½ cup finely chopped mushrooms
½ lb chicken livers, diced
1 tablespoon all-purpose flour
2 tablespoons Marsala
1¼ cups Brodo di Pollo (see page 19)
1 tablespoon tomato paste
4 slices bacon, cooked and crumbled
salt and pepper

Melt 3 tablespoons of the butter in a saucepan, add the onion and sauté for 6 to 8 minutes, stirring occasionally. Increase the heat and add the mushrooms and chicken livers; cook, stirring, for 2 minutes. Add the flour and cook, stirring, for 1 minute.

Add the Marsala, then stir in the stock, tomato paste, bacon and a little salt and pepper. Bring to a boil, cover and simmer for 30 to 40 minutes. Stir in the remaining butter and check the seasoning.

Serve hot with pasta, *Gnocchi di patate* (see page 76) or *Risotto alla paesana* (see page 29).
Serves 4

Salsa di Carne
Meat Sauce

4 slices bacon, diced
1 tablespoon butter
1 onion, chopped
1 carrot, diced
1 stalk celery, diced
¾ lb lean ground
    beef
2 tablespoons
    all-purpose flour
2 cups beef stock or
    broth
1 tablespoon tomato
    paste
salt and pepper
grated nutmeg

Cook the bacon in a saucepan until crisp. Add the butter, onion, carrot and celery and cook over low heat for 10 minutes, stirring frequently. Add the meat and cook, stirring, until browned. Stir in the flour and cook for 2 minutes.

Stir in the stock and tomato paste, and season to taste with salt, pepper and nutmeg. Bring to a boil, cover and simmer for 1 hour, stirring occasionally.

Serve with pasta.

Serves 4 to 6

Ragù Bolognese
Rich Meat Sauce

4 slices bacon, diced
1 tablespoon butter
1 onion, finely
    chopped
1 carrot, diced
1 stalk celery, diced
¾ lb lean ground
    beef
¼ lb chicken livers,
    chopped
¼ cup dry vermouth
    or white wine
1¼ cups beef stock or
    broth
1 tablespoon tomato
    paste
salt and pepper
grated nutmeg
2 tablespoons light
    cream

Cook the bacon in a saucepan until crisp, add the butter, onion, carrot and celery and cook over low heat for 10 minutes, stirring frequently. Add the meat and cook, stirring, until browned. Stir in the chicken livers and vermouth. Bring to a boil and cook until the liquid has almost completely evaporated.

Stir in the stock and tomato paste and season to taste with salt, pepper and nutmeg. Bring to a boil, cover and simmer for 1 hour, stirring occasionally. Check the seasoning and stir in the cream.

Serve with tagliatelli, spaghetti or other pasta.

Serves 4 to 6

Salsa di Pomodori
Tomato Sauce (using canned tomatoes)

1 can (16 oz)
    crushed tomatoes
1 onion, chopped
1 clove garlic,
    crushed
1 carrot, sliced
1 stalk celery, diced
2 teaspoons tomato
    paste
1 teaspoon sugar
salt and pepper
2 teaspoons chopped
    basil

Place the tomatoes, onion, garlic, carrot, celery, tomato paste and sugar in a saucepan. Stir in salt and pepper to taste. Bring to a boil, partially cover and simmer for 30 minutes.

Process in a blender or food processor, then return to the pan. Stir in the basil and check the seasoning.

Serve as required, with pasta or meat dishes.

Makes about 1¼ cups

Salsa Pizzaiola
Fresh Tomato Sauce

2 tablespoons olive
  oil
2 cloves garlic,
  crushed
1½ lb ripe tomatoes,
  peeled and chopped
1 teaspoon sugar
salt and pepper
1 tablespoon chopped
  basil, oregano or
  parsley

Heat the oil in a saucepan, add the
garlic and cook until softened, about
2 minutes. Add the tomatoes, sugar
and salt and pepper to taste. Cook
briskly for a few minutes until most
of the liquid has evaporated and the
tomatoes are softened.

Garnish with the herbs and use as
desired with steaks, chops, fish or
pasta.
Serves 4

15

Besciamella
Béchamel Sauce

3 tablespoons butter
6 tablespoons
    all-purpose flour
2½ cups hot milk
salt and pepper
grated nutmeg
    (optional)

Melt the butter in a saucepan, add the flour and cook, stirring, for 1 minute. Remove from the heat and gradually stir in the milk.

Return to the heat and cook, stirring, until thickened. Simmer for 3 minutes. Season with salt, pepper and nutmeg to taste.

Makes about 2½ cups

NOTE: For additional flavor, add a bay leaf to the milk before heating. Remove before adding the milk to the sauce.

Maionese
Mayonnaise

2 large egg yolks
½ teaspoon salt
2-3 teaspoons lemon
    juice
¾-1 cup olive oil

Have all the ingredients at room temperature.

Beat the egg yolks in a small bowl, add the salt and 1 teaspoon of the lemon juice and beat. Add the oil drop by drop, beating constantly, until the sauce becomes thick and shiny. Add the rest of the oil in a thin stream, beating constantly. Add lemon juice to taste.

Makes about 1¼ cups

Maionese Tonnata
Tuna Fish Mayonnaise

1 cup Maionese (see
  opposite page)
1 can (3½ oz) tuna
  fish
3 anchovy fillets
1 tablespoon lemon
  juice

Place the mayonnaise in the container
of a blender or food processor. Add
the remaining ingredients and
process until smooth.

Use over hard-cooked eggs, sliced
cold chicken, turkey or veal.
Makes about 1¼ cups

Salsa Verde
Piquant Green Sauce

2 shallots
1 clove garlic
1 gherkin
1 tablespoon capers
½ cup chopped
  parsley
2 tablespoons lemon
  juice
6 tablespoons olive
  oil
salt and pepper

Place all the ingredients in the
container of a blender or food
processor and process until smooth.
                OR
Finely chop the first five ingredients
together. Stir in the lemon juice and
oil, and season to taste with salt and
pepper.

Serve with hot or cold boiled
meat, fish or poultry.
Makes about 1 cup

Stracciatella
Roman Egg Soup

2 eggs
*2 tablespoons fine
    semolina*
*½ cup grated
    Parmesan cheese*
*6 cups Brodo di Pollo
    (see opposite page)*

Beat together the eggs, semolina, cheese and about 1 cup of the *Brodo di Pollo* (chicken broth). Bring the remaining broth to a boil in a saucepan, immediately remove from the heat and beat in the egg mixture.

Continue beating over low heat for 2 to 3 minutes or just until the eggs break into "ragged" flakes. Serve immediately.
Serves 4 to 6

Brodo di Pollo
Chicken Broth

This forms the basis of many soups and sauces. The chicken can be served hot for the main course, or cold with *Salsa verde* or *Maionese tonnata* (see page 17).

1 3-4 lb stewing
   chicken
2 quarts water
1 carrot, sliced
1 onion, sliced
2 stalks celery, sliced
2 tomatoes, quartered
1 bay leaf
6 peppercorns
1 teaspoon salt

Place the chicken and giblets (except the liver) in a stock pot and add the water. Bring to a boil and skim off any scum. Add the vegetables, bay leaf, peppercorns and salt. Cover and simmer gently for about 2 hours or until the chicken is tender. Remove the chicken. Strain the broth and check the seasoning.

Makes about 2 quarts

Passatelli in Brodo
Cheese Noodles in Broth

5 cups Brodo di Pollo
(see page 19)
1 egg, beaten
2 teaspoons
all-purpose flour
1/4 cup grated
Parmesan cheese
1/3 cup dry white
bread crumbs
1 tablespoon butter,
softened
pepper
grated nutmeg

Bring the *Brodo di Pollo* (chicken broth) to a boil in a large saucepan.

Place the egg, flour, cheese, bread crumbs and butter in a bowl. Add pepper and nutmeg to taste and work to a firm paste.

Press through a food mill or metal colander directly into the boiling broth. Simmer until the noodles rise to the surface, about 2 minutes.

Pour into individual soup bowls and serve immediately, with extra Parmesan cheese.

Serves 4 to 6

Zuppa di Zucchini
Zucchini Soup

3 tablespoons butter
1 onion, sliced
1 lb zucchini, thinly
sliced
5 cups Brodo di Pollo
(see page 19)
2 small eggs
2 tablespoons grated
Parmesan cheese
1 tablespoon chopped
parsley
2 teaspoons chopped
basil
salt and pepper
GARNISH:
crostini (see right)

Melt the butter in a large saucepan, add the onion and sauté for 5 minutes. Add the zucchini and cook, stirring frequently, for 5 to 10 minutes. Add the chicken broth, bring to a boil, cover and simmer for 20 minutes.

Process in a blender or food processor. Return to the saucepan and bring back to a boil.

Beat the eggs, cheese and herbs together in a bowl, then slowly stir in the boiling soup. Check the seasoning, and ladle into individual soup bowls. Garnish with crostini and serve immediately.

Serves 4 to 6

CROSTINI: Toast bread slices on one side in a hot oven. Spread the untoasted side with butter, sprinkle with grated cheese and place under a hot broiler until golden and bubbling. Cut into cubes.

Minestra di Frittata

Omelet Soup

5 cups *Brodo di Pollo*
  (see page 19)
2 eggs
1 tablespoon
  all-purpose flour
¼ cup milk
salt and pepper
¼ cup grated
  Parmesan cheese
chopped parsley for
  garnish

Bring the *Brodo di Pollo* (chicken broth) to a boil in a large saucepan.

Beat the eggs with the flour, milk and a little salt and pepper.

Heat a little oil in a large skillet and place over high heat. When very hot, pour in the batter and cook for about 1 minute or until set. Tip out of the pan, roll up and cut into thin strips. Add to the boiling broth with the cheese.

Serve immediately, sprinkled with parsley.
Serves 4 to 6

Minestrone
Thick Vegetable Soup

½ lb cabbage
1 large onion
1 large carrot
2 stalks celery
2 zucchini
3 tomatoes, peeled
4 slices bacon
2 tablespoons oil
2 cloves garlic,
    crushed
2 quarts water
4 basil leaves,
    chopped
½ cup rice
2 tablespoons
    chopped parsley
2 tablespoons grated
    Parmesan cheese
salt and pepper

Shred the cabbage; chop the other vegetables and the bacon. Heat the oil in a large saucepan, add the bacon, onion, carrot, celery and garlic and cook gently, stirring frequently, for about 10 minutes.

Add the water, bring to a boil and add the cabbage, zucchini, tomatoes, basil and rice. Continue cooking gently for 20 minutes.

Stir in the parsley, cheese and salt and pepper to taste.

Serve with extra Parmesan cheese and crusty bread.

Serves 6

NOTE: Small pasta may be used instead of rice.

Antipasti Misti

3 tomatoes, sliced
3 tablespoons olive
    oil
1 teaspoon chopped
    basil
salt and pepper
1 fennel bulb
1 teaspoon lemon
    juice
1 clove garlic,
    crushed
6 slices Italian salami
6 slices garlic sausage
½ cup ripe olives
2 hard-cooked eggs,
    quartered
basil or parsley sprigs
    for garnish

Arrange the tomato slices at one end of a large oval platter and sprinkle with 1 tablespoon of the oil, the basil and salt and pepper to taste.

Trim the fennel, cut lengthwise into thin slices, then into strips. Mix the remaining oil with the lemon juice, garlic and salt and pepper to taste. Add the fennel and toss well. Arrange at the other end of the platter.

Arrange the salami and garlic sausage in the middle of the platter. Top with the olives and surround with the eggs. Garnish with basil or parsley.

Serves 4

Antipasto alla Casalinga

2 green peppers
3 tablespoons olive oil
2 teaspoons red wine vinegar
salt and pepper
4 tomatoes, sliced
few thinly sliced onion rings
1 can (7 oz) tuna fish, drained and flaked
2 cans (3¾ oz each) sardines in oil, drained

TO SERVE:
¼ cup Maionese (see page 16)

Cook the peppers under a preheated broiler until the skin is charred and blistered, turning frequently. Cut in half and rinse under cold water to remove the skin and seeds. Pat dry and finely slice. Mix with 2 tablespoons of the oil, the vinegar and a little salt. Chill in the refrigerator until required.

Season the tomato slices with salt and pepper to taste and sprinkle with the remaining oil. Arrange the pepper slices on a large serving platter and top with the tomatoes. Scatter the onion rings over the top.

Place the tuna fish in the center and surround with the sardines. Serve with mayonnaise.
Serves 4

Carciofi alla Borghese
Marinated Artichoke Hearts

1 clove garlic, crushed
1½ tablespoons
   lemon juice
4½ tablespoons olive
   oil
salt and pepper
1 bay leaf
16 fresh cooked or
   canned artichoke
   hearts
1 tablespoon chopped
   parsley

Beat together the garlic, lemon juice, oil and salt and pepper to taste in a bowl. Add the bay leaf and artichoke hearts and stir gently. Cover and chill for about 2 hours, stirring occasionally. Discard the bay leaf.

Divide the artichokes between individual dishes, spoon the marinade over and sprinkle with parsley.
Serves 4

Caponata
Eggplant Appetizer

1 large eggplant
salt and pepper
4 stalks celery
6 tablespoons olive
   oil
1 large onion,
   chopped
1 can (16 oz)
   crushed tomatoes
1 tablespoon tomato
   paste
2-3 tablespoons red
   wine vinegar
2 tablespoons sugar
2 tablespoons capers
12 pitted green olives
GARNISH:
1 tablespoon pignoli
   or sliced almonds
2 hard-cooked eggs,
   quartered

Cut the eggplant into ½ inch cubes. Sprinkle with salt, place in a colander and let stand for 1 hour. Pat dry with paper towels.

Cook the celery in boiling water for 6 to 8 minutes. Drain and cut into ½ inch cubes.

Heat 4 tablespoons of the oil in a large skillet, add the eggplant and sauté quickly, stirring frequently, for about 10 minutes or until tender. Season to taste with salt and pepper.

Heat the remaining oil in a large saucepan, add the onion and sauté for 5 minutes. Add the celery and cook, stirring, for 5 minutes. Add the tomatoes, tomato paste and a little salt and pepper. Simmer gently for about 5 minutes or until the celery and onion are tender.

Add 2 tablespoons vinegar, the sugar, capers, olives and eggplant. Simmer for a few minutes, stirring. Adjust the seasoning and add extra vinegar if necessary. Cool, cover and chill until required. Garnish with pignoli and egg wedges.
Serves 4 to 6

Insalata di Funghi e Gamberi
Raw Mushroom and Shrimp Salad

6 tablespoons olive
  oil
2 tablespoons lemon
  juice
pepper
1 clove garlic, crushed
¾ lb mushrooms,
  thinly sliced
½ teaspoon salt
1 tablespoon chopped
  parsley
½ lb shelled cooked
  tiny shrimp

Beat the oil, lemon juice and a little
pepper together in a bowl. Add the
garlic and mushrooms and stir
gently. Cover and chill for at least 1
hour.

Stir in the salt and parsley. Spoon
into a serving dish and top with the
shrimp.
Serves 4

NOTE: Very fresh mushrooms and
good olive oil are essential for this
recipe.

Uova Sode Tonnata
Eggs with Tuna Mayonnaise

4 hard-cooked eggs
Maionese Tonnata
(see page 17)
4 anchovy fillets
few capers
parsley sprigs for
garnish

Cut the eggs in half lengthwise and arrange cut side down on individual dishes. Coat with tuna mayonnaise.

Cut the anchovy fillets in half lengthwise and curl one strip on top of each egg half. Sprinkle with capers and garnish with parsley.
Serves 4

Prosciutto con Melone
Prosciutto with Melon

1 sweet ripe melon,
chilled
4 slices prosciutto

Cut the melon into quarters and remove the seeds. Wrap the slices of prosciutto over the melon. Serve with freshly ground black pepper.
Serves 4

Prosciutto e Fichi
Prosciutto with Figs

8 ripe figs
4 slices prosciutto

Cut the figs into quarters almost to the bottom. Arrange the ham on individual plates and top with figs.
Serves 4

Risotto con Ragù
Rice with Meat Sauce

1½ cups Brodo di
  Pollo (see page
  19)
1 tablespoon oil
4 tablespoons butter
1 onion, finely
  chopped
1⅓ cups pre-cooked
  rice
¼ cup grated
  Parmesan cheese
salt and pepper
Salsa di Carne or
  Salsa de Fegatini
  (see pages 12-13)

Place the chicken broth in a saucepan and bring to a boil.

Heat the oil and half the butter in a heavy saucepan, add the onion and sauté until soft. Add the rice and cook, stirring, for 1 minute.

Add the hot broth, stir well and remove from the heat. Let stand for 5 minutes. Stir in the remaining butter, the cheese, and salt and pepper to taste and fluff with a fork.

Spoon into a warmed serving dish and serve with sauce and extra Parmesan cheese.
Serves 4

Risotto alla Paesana
Country-Style Rice

3 tablespoons olive oil
1 onion, chopped
2 stalks celery, thinly sliced
1 zucchini, thinly sliced
½ pkg (10 oz) frozen lima beans
1½ cups Brodo di Pollo (see page 19)
1⅓ cups pre-cooked rice
2 tablespoons butter
¼ lb cooked ham, cut into strips
¼ cup grated Parmesan cheese
salt and pepper

Heat the oil in a heavy-based saucepan, add the onion and celery and sauté for 3 minutes. Stir in the zucchini and beans, cover and cook gently for 5 minutes. Add the broth and bring to a boil.

Stir in the rice. Cover and remove from the heat. Let stand for 10 minutes or until the liquid is absorbed. Fluff with a fork. Stir in the butter, ham, cheese and salt and pepper to taste.

Spoon onto a warmed serving dish and serve immediately, with extra Parmesan cheese.
Serves 4

Pasta all' Uovo
Homemade Egg Pasta

2 cups all-purpose
  flour
2 large eggs
2 teaspoons oil
½ teaspoon salt
3 tablespoons water
  (approximately)

Sift the flour into a mound on a work surface and make a well in the center. Put the eggs, oil and salt into the well and mix together with the fingers. Gradually work in the flour to form a crumbly dough. Knead to a firm but pliable dough, adding water as necessary.

Knead for 10 minutes or until smooth and elastic. Cover with a piece of oiled plastic wrap and leave to rest for 1 hour.

Roll out the dough on a lightly floured surface, rotating the dough a quarter turn after every roll until the dough is ⅛ inch thick. Shape and use as required (see below).

Pasta Verdi (Green Pasta)
Follow the above recipe, adding ½ pkg (10 oz) frozen chopped spinach, (cooked and squeezed dry) with the eggs. This pasta is softer than plain pasta and frequent flouring of the work surface may be neccesary.

Shaping Pasta

Stuffed Pasta: The dough should be used immediately, without drying.

Flat and Ribbon Pasta: Dust the dough lightly with flour and let dry for 15 to 20 minutes, but do not allow to become brittle. Cut flat pasta into shapes as illustrated. Roll ribbon pasta into a loose jelly roll and cut across into strips as illustrated.

Cooking Pasta

Homemade Pasta: Place the pasta in a large pot containing 3 to 4 quarts boiling water and 1½ tablespoons salt. Stir well, then boil steadily, uncovered, for 3 to 5 minutes or until *al dente* – just tender but firm to the bite. Test frequently to avoid overcooking, as pasta continues to soften until you eat it. The moment it is done, thoroughly drain the pasta in a colander and serve immediately.

Dry Pasta: As above, but follow the package directions because cooking times are longer for dry pastas and vary considerably for different shapes and brands.

Never break up long pasta such as spaghetti; simply bend it into the pan as it softens.

Quantities

Allow 3 to 4 oz pasta per person for a main course, 2 oz for a first course.

Tagliolini con Tonno

1 can (7 oz) tuna
  fish
1 clove garlic,
  crushed
2 tablespoons
  chopped parsley
½ lb ripe tomatoes,
  peeled and
  chopped
⅔ cup chicken stock
salt and pepper
¾ lb tagliolini

Drain the oil from the tuna into a
saucepan, add the garlic and cook for
2 minutes. Add the parsley and
tomatoes and cook until the
tomatoes begin to soften. Flake the
tuna and add to the saucepan with
the stock and salt and pepper to taste.
Simmer while cooking the pasta.

Cook the pasta in boiling salted
water until *al dente*; drain well. Place
in a warmed serving dish. Add the
sauce, toss and serve immediately.
Serves 4

Spaghetti alla Carbonara

¾ lb spaghetti
salt and pepper
½ lb bacon, chopped
3 eggs
3 tablespoons heavy
  cream
½ cup grated
  Parmesan cheese
3 tablespoons butter

Cook the spaghetti in boiling salted
water until *al dente*.

Meanwhile, cook the bacon until
crisp. Drain well.

Beat the eggs with the cream,
cheese, a little salt and plenty of
pepper. Melt the butter in a large
saucepan, add the egg mixture and
stir until just beginning to thicken.
Add the drained spaghetti and bacon,
mix well and serve immediately.
Serves 4

Fettuccine al Gorgonzola

1 pkg (12 oz)
  fettuccine
salt and pepper
2 tablespoons butter
5 tablespoons milk
¼ lb Gorgonzola
  cheese, diced
½ cup heavy cream
¼ cup grated
  Parmesan cheese
1-2 tablespoons
  chopped basil
  (optional)

Cook the pasta in boiling salted
water until *al dente*.

Meanwhile, put the butter, milk
and Gorgonzola cheese into a
flameproof casserole. Place over a
moderate heat and mash the cheese
to a creamy sauce. Add the cream,
and salt and pepper to taste and heat
to simmering point.

Stir in the drained pasta, Parmesan
cheese and basil if using. Toss until
the pasta is coated, then serve
immediately with extra Parmesan
cheese.
Serves 4

Lasagne al Forno

½ lb spinach lasagne
salt
2 cups Ragù
    Bolognese (see
    page 14)
2½ cups Besciamella
    (see page 16)
⅓ cup grated
    Parmesan cheese

Cook the lasagne in boiling salted
water until *al dente*. Drain, rinse
under cold water, spread on clean
dish towels and pat dry.

Butter an 8 inch square baking
dish, at least 1½ inches deep. Spread
a layer of *Ragù* (meat sauce) on the
bottom, cover with a layer of
lasagne, then a layer of *Ragù* and
finish with a thin layer of *Besciamella*
(béchamel sauce) and a sprinkling of
cheese. Repeat these layers twice,
finishing with cheese.

Bake in a preheated 400°F oven for
20 to 25 minutes or until golden and
bubbling. Serve immediately.
Serves 4 to 6

Tagliatelle alla Bolognese

¾ lb spinach
    tagliatelle
salt
2 tablespoons butter
2 cups hot Ragù
    Bolognese (see
    page 14)
2 tablespoons grated
    Parmesan cheese

Cook the tagliatelle in boiling salted
water until *al dente*. Drain thoroughly.

Melt the butter and pour into a
deep serving dish. Add 4 tablespoons
of the *Ragù* (meat sauce), the pasta
and Parmesan cheese. Toss lightly
until the pasta is coated. Spoon the
remaining sauce on top and pass
more cheese separately.
Serves 4

Cannelloni

12 flat pieces home-
    made pasta, about
    3 × 4 inches each
salt and pepper
2 cups Besciamella
    (see page 16)
1¼ cups Salsa di
    Pomodori (see
    page 14)
3 tablespoons grated
    Parmesan cheese
2 tablespoons butter
FILLING:
2 tablespoons oil
1 onion, chopped
1 clove garlic,
    crushed
½ lb lean ground
    beef
1 pkg (10 oz) frozen
    chopped spinach,
    cooked and
    squeezed dry
⅓ cup grated
    Parmesan cheese
1 egg yolk

Cook the pasta in boiling salted
water until *al dente*, stirring
occasionally. Drain, spread on a
clean dish-towel and pat dry.

To prepare the filling, heat the oil
in a saucepan, add the onion and
garlic and sauté until softened. Add
the meat and cook, stirring, until
well browned. Stir in the remaining
ingredients. Bind the mixture with
2 tablespoons of the *Besciamella*
(béchamel sauce) and season well
with salt and pepper.

Spread a heaped tablespoon of
filling over each piece of pasta. Roll
up loosely from the narrow side and
place, seam side down, in a buttered
8 inch square baking dish.

Pour the *Salsa di pomodori* (tomato
sauce) over and cover with the
Besciamella. Sprinkle with the cheese
and dot with the butter.

Bake in a preheated 400°F oven for
15 to 20 minutes or until golden and
bubbling.
Serves 6

Macaroni con Pomodori
Savory Baked Macaroni

2 tablespoons oil
1 large onion, finely
  chopped
2 cloves garlic,
  crushed
1 small chili pepper,
  seeded and finely
  chopped
1 can (16 oz)
  crushed tomatoes
4 slices bacon, cooked
  and crumbled
1 teaspoon sugar
salt
½ lb elbow macaroni
½ cup grated
  Provolone or other
  hard cheese

Heat the oil in a saucepan, add the onion, garlic and chili pepper and sauté until softened, stirring occasionally. Add the tomatoes, bacon, sugar and salt to taste. Bring to a boil, stirring, cover and simmer for 20 minutes.

Cook the macaroni in boiling salted water until *al dente*; drain thoroughly.

Arrange alternate layers of pasta, sauce and cheese in a greased baking dish, finishing with cheese.

Serve immediately, or cover and heat in a preheated 275°F oven for 20 to 30 minutes to allow the flavors to blend.

Serves 3 to 4

Crespelle Ripiene
Spinach and Cheese Stuffed Crêpes

CRÊPE BATTER:
1 cup all-purpose
  flour
¼ teaspoon salt
2 small eggs
1 tablespoon olive oil
  oil
¾ cup milk
6-8 tablespoons
  water

FILLING:
1 pkg (10 oz) frozen
  chopped spinach,
  cooked and
  squeezed dry
1 cup Ricotta cheese
¼ cup grated
  Parmesan cheese
1 egg, beaten
grated nutmeg
salt and pepper

TOPPING:
2 tablespoons butter
  or margarine
3 tablespoons grated
  Parmesan cheese
5 tablespoons chicken
  stock or broth

Sift the flour and salt into a bowl. Make a well in the center and add the eggs, oil and milk. Beat until smooth, then stir in the water. Cover and chill for 1 to 2 hours.

Lightly oil a 7 inch crêpe pan and place over moderate heat. When hot, pour in just enough batter to cover the bottom. When the crêpe is set and the underside lightly browned, turn and briefly cook the other side. Repeat with the remaining batter, making eight crêpes.

Mix the filling ingredients together, seasoning liberally with nutmeg, salt and pepper. Divide between the crêpes, roll up loosely and arrange in a buttered baking dish. Dot with the butter, sprinkle with the Parmesan cheese and pour in the stock.

Bake in a preheated 400°F oven, for about 20 minutes or until golden. Serve immediately.
Serves 4

Pizza alla Casalinga
Home-Style Pizza

PIZZA DOUGH:

1 pkg (¼ oz) active dry yeast
2 tablespoons warm water
2 cups all-purpose flour
1 teaspoon salt
2 tablespoons olive oil
6 tablespoons milk (approximately)

TOPPING:

3 tablespoons olive oil
1 lb tomatoes, peeled, seeded and chopped
1 teaspoon dried oregano or basil
salt and pepper
½ lb Mozzarella cheese, sliced
¼ cup grated Parmesan cheese
6-8 ripe olives

Dissolve the yeast in the warm water. Sift the flour and salt into a bowl, make a well in the center and pour in the yeast, oil and milk. Mix to a firm but pliable dough, adding a little more milk if necessary.

Place on a floured surface and knead vigorously for 5 minutes. Place in a greased bowl, cover and let rise in a warm place until doubled in bulk.

Knead the dough lightly, then cut in half. Roll out each piece into an 8 to 9 inch round.

Place the rounds on oiled cookie sheets and brush with some of the oil. Cover with the tomatoes and sprinkle with the herbs and salt and pepper to taste. Add the Mozzarella slices, then top with the Parmesan and olives.

Spoon the remaining oil over and let rise in a warm place for 30 minutes.

Bake in a preheated 425°F oven for 25 to 30 minutes. Serve immediately.
Serves 4

38

Pizzette
Individual Pizzas

1 recipe Pizza dough
  (see opposite page)
TOPPING:
3 tablespoons olive
  oil
1 lb tomatoes,
  peeled, seeded and
  chopped
salt and pepper
1 cup sliced
  mushrooms,
  sautéed
2-3 cloves garlic,
  finely chopped
2-3 tablespoons
  grated Parmesan
  cheese

Divide the risen dough into six
portions, shape into balls and roll
into 4 inch rounds.

Brush with half of the oil, cover
with the tomatoes and season well.

Top with the mushrooms, garlic
and cheese. Sprinkle with the
remaining oil and let rise in a warm
place for about 15 minutes.

Bake in a preheated 425°F oven for
about 15 minutes. Serve
immediately.
Serves 6
ALTERNATIVE TOPPINGS:
1. Chopped salami and ripe olives.
2. Sliced peppers, diced Mozzarella
cheese and anchovy fillets.

Sardenara
San Remo Pizza

1 recipe Pizza dough
  (see opposite page)
TOPPING:
7 tablespoons olive
  oil
3 medium-size
  onions, thinly
  sliced
1-2 cloves garlic,
  crushed
1 can (16 oz)
  crushed tomatoes
1 teaspoon dried
  oregano
salt and pepper
1 can (2 oz) anchovy
  fillets, cut into
  strips
20 ripe olives

To make the topping, heat
4 tablespoons of the oil in a
saucepan, add the onions and sauté
until soft and golden. Add the garlic,
tomatoes, oregano and a little salt
and pepper. Cook, uncovered, until
reduced and thickened. Check the
seasoning and let cool.

Place the risen dough on a floured
surface and knead lightly. Cut in
half, shape each into a ball and place
in well oiled 8 to 9 inch foil pie pans.
Press out the dough to cover the
bottom of the pans and to reach
½ inch up the sides. Brush with
1 tablespoon oil.

Spread the tomato mixture over
the dough and arrange the anchovy
strips and olives on top. Sprinkle the
remaining oil over.

Bake in a preheated 425°F oven for
25 to 30 minutes. Serve immediately.
Serves 4 to 6

FISH

Spiedini di Scampi
Broiled Jumbo Shrimp

1½ lb frozen jumbo
  shrimp, just
  thawed, shelled
  and dried
¼ cup olive oil
⅔ cup dry white
  bread crumbs
2-3 cloves garlic,
  crushed
1 tablespoon finely
  chopped parsley
salt and pepper
lemon wedges
  to serve

Put the shrimp in a bowl with the oil, bread crumbs, garlic, parsley and salt and pepper to taste. Stir gently until thoroughly coated. Cover and marinate for 30 minutes.

Thread onto four kabob skewers, pushing the shrimp to the center. Broil for 2 to 3 minutes on each side, depending on size, until the crumbs are crisp. Serve immediately, with lemon wedges.
Serves 4

Pesce alla Griglia
Marinated Broiled Fish

4 small mackerel,
   whiting, trout or
   gray mullet,
   cleaned
salt and pepper
2 rosemary sprigs or
   bay leaves
¼ cup olive oil
1½ tablespoons
   lemon juice
1 small clove garlic,
   crushed (optional)
lemon wedges for
   garnish

Make three cuts across each side of the fish. Sprinkle with salt and pepper. Place the herbs in a shallow glass dish and lay the fish on top. Mix together the oil, lemon juice and garlic, if using, and pour over the fish. Cover and place in the refrigerator. Marinate for 3 to 4 hours, turning several times.

Place the fish in the broiler, about 4 inches from the source of the heat and cook for 5 to 6 minutes on each side or until cooked through.

Serve immediately, garnished with lemon wedges.
Serves 4

Sgombro en Cartoccio

Mackerel Packages

4 mackerel, about
    ½ lb each, cleaned
salt and pepper
3 tablespoons olive
    oil (approximately)
1 onion, finely
    chopped
2 stalks celery, finely
    chopped
1 tablespoon chopped
    parsley
1 clove garlic,
    crushed (optional)
½ teaspoon dried
    oregano or basil
juice of ½ lemon

Season the fish liberally with salt and pepper and brush with oil. Cut pieces of foil 2 inches longer and wider than the fish. Brush the foil lightly with oil.

Heat 2 tablespoons oil in a skillet, add the onion and celery and sauté for 10 minutes. Add the parsley, garlic, if using, dried herbs, lemon juice and a little salt and pepper to taste.

Lay a fish on each piece of foil and top with the vegetable mixture. Fold over the foil, sealing the edges well, to enclose the fish. Place on a cookie sheet and cook in a preheated 400°F oven for 25 to 30 minutes.

Serve the mackerel in the partially opened foil packages.
Serves 4

Pesce Gratinato al Forno
Golden Baked Fish

4 cod, hake or
    haddock steaks
salt and pepper
²/₃ cup dry white
    bread crumbs
¹/₂ cup grated
    Parmesan cheese
MARINADE:
¹/₄ cup olive oil
1 small clove garlic,
    crushed
2 mint or parsley
    sprigs, finely
    chopped
¹/₄ teaspoon dried
    oregano
GARNISH:
lemon quarters
parsley or mint sprigs

Combine the marinade ingredients in a shallow glass dish. Season the fish with salt and pepper and place in the marinade, turning to coat. Cover and place in the refrigerator. Marinate for 3 to 4 hours, turning once. Drain, reserving the marinade.

Mix together the bread crumbs and cheese and use to coat the fish, pressing on firmly.

Strain the marinade into a baking dish and add the fish. Spoon enough marinade over to moisten the coating. Cook in a preheated 375°F oven for 20 to 25 minutes. Garnish with lemon and herbs.

Serves 4

Trotelle alla Savoia
Trout with Mushrooms

flour for coating
salt and pepper
4 lake trout, cleaned
2 tablespoons oil
5 tablespoons butter
3 scallions (green
    part only),
    chopped
¾ lb button
    mushrooms
1 tablespoon lemon
    juice
1 tablespoon chopped
    parsley
⅓ cup dry white
    bread crumbs
lemon wedges for
    garnish

Season the flour with salt and pepper and use to coat the trout.

Heat the oil and 2 tablespoons of the butter in a large skillet. Add the trout and sauté for 6 minutes on each side or until cooked and golden.

Meanwhile, melt the remaining butter in a saucepan, add the scallions and mushrooms and sauté for 3 minutes or until the mushrooms begin to soften. Stir in the lemon juice, parsley and a little salt.

Arrange the trout and mushroom mixture on a warmed serving platter and keep hot.

Quickly sauté the bread crumbs in the butter remaining in the saucepan until crisp. Sprinkle over the fish and garnish with lemon wedges.
Serves 4

Sogliola all' Italiana
Sole with Zucchini

¼ cup oil
1 onion, finely
    chopped
½ lb tomatoes,
    peeled and
    chopped
1 teaspoon tomato
    paste
½ teaspoon dried
    basil
salt and pepper
4 small zucchini,
    thinly sliced
flour for coating
4 fillets of sole, about
    1½ lb
2 tablespoons butter
2 tablespoons grated
    Parmesan cheese

Heat half the oil in a saucepan, add the onion and sauté until soft. Add the tomatoes, tomato paste, basil and a little salt and pepper. Simmer, covered, for 5 minutes. Add the zucchini and simmer for 8 minutes longer or until just tender.

Season the flour with salt and pepper and use to coat the fish. Heat the remaining oil with the butter in a large skillet, add the fish and sauté for 5 to 6 minutes on each side or until cooked and golden.

Transfer to a shallow baking dish and top with the vegetable mixture. Sprinkle with the cheese and broil until lightly browned. Serve immediately.
Serves 4

Pesce alla Veneziana
Venetian-Style Red Snapper

5 tablespoons olive
    oil
1 large onion,
    chopped
1¼ cups dry white
    wine
1½ tablespoons wine
    vinegar
1-2 mint sprigs
2 cloves garlic,
    chopped
4 red snapper,
    cleaned
salt and pepper
flour for coating
GARNISH:
orange and lemon
    slices
mint sprigs

Heat 2 tablespoons of the oil in a skillet, add the onion and sauté until soft but not colored. Add the wine and vinegar and boil briskly for 10 minutes or until reduced by half.

Meanwhile, put 2 or 3 mint leaves and a little garlic inside each fish. Season the flour well with salt and pepper and use to coat the fish.

Heat the remaining oil in a skillet, add the fish and sauté for about 6 minutes on each side or until crisp, golden and cooked through. Drain and arrange in a shallow dish. Pour the hot sauce over and cool, basting occasionally.

Serve cold, garnished with orange and lemon slices and mint.

Serves 4

Maionese di Pesce
Italian Fish Mayonnaise

1½ lb white fish
    fillet (e.g. cod,
    haddock,
    swordfish)
salt and pepper
1 lemon
3-4 tablespoons olive
    oil
1 pkg (10 oz) frozen
    mixed vegetables
½ cup cooked shelled
    tiny shrimp
¾ cup Maionese (see
    page 16)
GARNISH:
2 hard-cooked eggs,
    sliced
few stuffed olives,
    sliced
few capers (optional)

Put the fish in a saucepan and cover with cold water. Add 1 teaspoon salt and two lemon slices. Bring to simmering point and poach for 5 minutes or until cooked. Drain and chop the fish. While still hot, flavor to taste with oil, salt, pepper and lemon juice. Cover and let cool.

Cook the vegetables as directed on the package, drain and cool. Place on a serving plate and top with the fish and half the shrimp. Pour the mayonnaise over, thinning with water if necessary. Garnish with the remaining shrimp, the eggs, olives and capers, if using.

Serves 4

Petto di Vitello Ripieno
Stuffed Breast of Veal

---

1 boned breast of veal
    with pocket, about
    2 lb
2 tablespoons butter
STUFFING:
2 tablespoons oil
1 onion, chopped
1 pkg (10 oz) frozen
    chopped spinach,
    cooked and
    squeezed dry
½ lb pork sausage
1 egg, beaten
3 tablespoons grated
    Parmesan cheese
salt and pepper

To make the stuffing, heat the oil in a saucepan, add the onion and sauté until soft. Stir in the spinach, sausage, egg, cheese and salt and pepper to taste. Stuff the veal with the mixture and sew up the opening.

Place in a casserole and dot with the butter. Cover and cook in a preheated 325°F oven for 2 hours, turning once.

Remove the thread and slice the veal. Serve hot, with the pan juices poured over, or cold with salad.
Serves 6

Scaloppine alla Parmigiana
Veal Cutlets with Ham and Cheese

4 veal cutlets, about
  1 lb
flour for coating
salt and pepper
1 tablespoon oil
3 tablespoons butter
1 cup chopped
  proscuitto or
  cooked ham
2 tablespoons
  chopped parsley
¼ cup grated
  Parmesan cheese
¼ cup chicken stock
  or broth

Place each cutlet between two pieces of waxed paper and pound to flatten. Season the flour with salt and pepper and use to coat the veal.

Heat the oil and butter in a large skillet, add the veal and sauté for about 3 minutes on each side.

Mix the ham and parsley together and spread over the veal. Sprinkle with the cheese.

Stir the stock into the pan juices and spoon a little over each portion. Cover and cook gently for 5 minutes or until the veal is tender and the cheese melted.

Place in a warmed serving platter and keep hot. Bring the pan juices to a boil and cook until reduced. Pour over the veal and serve immediately.

Serves 4

Involtini di Vitello alla Neapolitana

Stuffed Veal Rolls

- 8 thinly cut veal cutlets, about 1 lb
- 8 thin slices cooked ham
- 1/2 cup soft bread crumbs, soaked in milk and squeezed dry
- 3 tablespoons golden raisins
- 1/4 cup pignoli or blanched sliced almonds
- 1/4 cup grated Parmesan cheese
- 2 tablespoons chopped parsley
- salt and pepper
- 1 tablespoon olive oil
- 2 tablespoons butter
- 3/4 cup dry white wine
- parsley sprigs for garnish

Place each cutlet between two pieces of waxed paper and pound to flatten. Cover each cutlet with a slice of ham.

Mix together the bread crumbs, raisins, nuts, cheese and parsley, and season to taste with salt and pepper. Divide between the cutlets, roll up and secure each one with a toothpick.

Heat the oil and butter in a skillet, add the veal rolls and sauté until lightly browned. Pour in the wine, cover and cook very gently, turning once, for 20 to 25 minutes or until tender.

Place the rolls on a warmed serving platter and keep hot. Bring the pan juices to a boil, stirring, and cook until well reduced. Spoon over the meat, garnish with parsley and serve immediately.

Serves 4

Vitello Tonnata
Veal with Tuna Fish Mayonnaise

1 boneless veal
   shoulder roast,
   about 2 lb
1 carrot, halved
1 onion, halved
1 stalk celery, sliced
1 bay leaf
4 peppercorns
salt
1¼ cups Maionese
   Tonnata (see page
   17)
GARNISH:
strips of anchovy
   fillets
capers
few ripe olives
thin lemon slices

Put the meat into a saucepan just
large enough to hold it. Add the
carrot, onion, celery, bay leaf,
peppercorns and 1 teaspoon salt. Add
just enough water to cover and bring
slowly to a boil. Skim the surface,
cover and simmer for 1½ to 2 hours
or until tender. Let cool in the stock.

Drain the meat and slice. Spread
half the Maionese Tonnata (tuna fish
mayonnaise) on a serving platter and
arrange the meat slices on top.
Spread the remainder of the
mayonnaise over the meat, covering
it completely.

Cover the platter loosely with foil
and chill in the refrigerator
overnight.

Garnish with anchovies, capers,
olives and lemon slices. Serve as an
antipasto or main course.
Serves 4 to 6

Bistecca alla Pizzaiola
Steaks with Tomato and Garlic Sauce

4 cube steaks
olive oil
salt and pepper
Salsa Pizzaiola (see page 15)
chopped herbs for garnish

Brush the steaks with oil and season with pepper to taste.

Lightly oil a skillet and place over moderate heat. When hot, add the steaks and panfry quickly for 2 minutes on each side.

Spread the steaks with the sauce, cover the skillet and cook over low heat for 5 to 10 minutes or until tender.

Transfer to a warmed serving platter, season with salt and garnish with herbs. Serve immediately.
Serves 4

Stufatino alla Romana
Roman-Style Beef Stew

3 tablespoons butter
1 small onion, finely chopped
¼ cup finely chopped cooked ham
1 stalk celery, diced
1 clove garlic, sliced
1½ lb beef for stew
¼ teaspoon dried marjoram
salt and pepper
1 cup dry red wine
1½-2 cups beef stock or broth
1 tablespoon tomato paste
TO SERVE:
1 large head celery, trimmed and cut into 2 inch lengths

Melt the butter in a skillet, add the onion and sauté until transparent. Add the ham, celery and garlic and cook for 1 minute. Add the meat, marjoram and salt and pepper to taste. Cook, stirring frequently, for 2 minutes.

Add the wine, bring to a boil and simmer until reduced by half. Add 1½ cups of the stock and the tomato paste. Cover and cook very gently for 3 to 4 hours or until the meat is tender and the sauce is thick and rich. Stir occasionally and add the remaining stock a little at a time during cooking if the sauce reduces too quickly.

Meanwhile, cook the celery in boiling salted water for 15 to 20 minutes or until tender. Drain and add to the stew just before serving, or serve separately.
Serves 4

Stracotto
Beef Braised in Wine

1 tablespoon oil
2 tablespoons butter
1 small onion,
  chopped
1 small carrot,
  chopped
1 stalk celery,
  chopped
1 beef round eye
  round roast, about
  3 lb
1 cup dry red wine
1 cup beef stock or
  broth
1 tablespoon tomato
  paste
1 thyme sprig
1 bay leaf
salt and pepper

Heat the oil and butter in a flameproof casserole, add the onion, carrot and celery and sauté for 5 minutes, stirring occasionally.

Add the meat and brown quickly on all sides. Add the wine, bring to a boil and simmer until well reduced.

Add the stock, tomato paste, herbs and salt and pepper to taste. Bring to simmering point, cover and cook in a preheated 300°F oven for 3 hours or until tender.

Slice the meat thickly, arrange on a warmed serving platter and keep hot.

Discard the herbs from the casserole. If necessary, reduce the sauce to about ½ cup by boiling uncovered, stirring frequently. Check the seasoning and spoon the sauce over the meat.
Serves 8

Fettine di Maiale alla Sorrentina

Sorrento-Style Pork Slices

2 tablespoons oil
1 clove garlic, halved
4 pork loin chops
salt and pepper
1 large green pepper,
    seeded and thinly
    sliced
1 can (8 oz)
    tomatoes
½ lb mushrooms,
    thinly sliced

Heat the oil and garlic in a large skillet. When the garlic browns, discard it.

Add the chops to the skillet and brown lightly on each side. Season with pepper to taste. Cover and cook very gently for 15 minutes. Remove from the skillet and keep hot.

Add the green pepper and tomatoes, with their juice, to the pan, stirring to break up the tomatoes. Cover and cook gently for 15 minutes.

Stir in the mushrooms and salt and pepper to taste. Cover and cook for 5 minutes.

Return the chops to the skillet, baste with the sauce and simmer until hot and cooked through. Serve the chops with the sauce spooned over.

Serves 4

Maiale alla Veneziana
Herbed Pork

1 3 lb boneless pork
 loin
1 clove garlic,
 crushed
3 sage leaves,
 chopped
2 rosemary sprigs,
 chopped
2 basil leaves,
 chopped
salt and pepper
2 tablespoons oil
2 cups Brodo di Pollo
 (see page 19)
2 teaspoons
 cornstarch,
 dissolved in 1
 tablespoon water

Untie the meat and open out flat.
Combine the garlic, sage, rosemary
and basil and spread over the inside
of the meat. Season well with salt
and pepper. Reroll the meat tightly
and secure with string. Rub the
outside wish salt and pepper.

Heat the oil in a Dutch oven or
deep flameproof casserole. Add the
meat and brown on all sides. Bring
chicken broth to a boil and slowly
pour over the meat. Cover and simmer for 2 hours or until the internal
temperature of the pork is 170°F.

Remove the pork to a warmed
serving platter. Skim off excess fat
from the cooking liquid. Stir in the
cornstarch and cook over low heat,
stirring, until slightly thickened.
Carve the meat into thick slices and
spoon the sauce over to serve.
Serves 4

Abbacchio Brodettato

Lamb in Lemon Sauce

2 tablespoons butter
½ cup chopped
  cooked ham
1½ lb boneless lamb
  for stew
1 onion, chopped
2 tablespoons
  all-purpose flour
salt and pepper
¼ cup dry white
  wine or vermouth
1½ cups chicken
  stock or broth
2 egg yolks
½ teaspoon finely
  grated lemon rind
2 tablespoons lemon
  juice
1 teaspoon chopped
  marjoram
1 tablespoon chopped
  parsley

Melt the butter in a heavy saucepan, add the ham, lamb and onion and sauté for 10 minutes, stirring frequently. Sprinkle in the flour and season to taste with salt and pepper. Cook, stirring, for 1 minute.

Add the wine or vermouth, bring to a boil and boil until reduced by half. Add the stock and bring back to a boil, stirring. Cover and simmer for 45 minutes or until the lamb is tender. Skim off any surface fat.

Beat together the egg yolks, lemon rind and juice and herbs. Add 3 tablespoons of the cooking liquid and blend well. Add to the pan and stir just until the sauce thickens; do not allow to boil. Check the seasoning and serve with noodles or new potatoes.

Serves 4

Abbacchio al Forno

Roast Lamb with Rosemary

1 leg of lamb, about
  3 lb
2-4 cloves garlic,
  sliced
3-4 rosemary sprigs
salt and pepper
1 tablespoon oil
⅔ cup dry white
  wine or chicken
  stock
rosemary sprigs for
  garnish

Make small incisions in the lamb and insert a piece of garlic and a few rosemary leaves into each. Season with salt and pepper and place on a rack in a roasting pan. Spoon the oil over.

Cook in a preheated 350°F oven for about 2 hours. Place on a warmed serving platter and keep hot.

Skim the fat from the pan juices, add the wine or stock and bring to a boil, stirring, until thickened. Strain into a sauceboat and serve with the meat.

Serves 6

Agnello Piccante
Piquant Lamb Chops

8 shoulder lamb
   chops
¼ cup olive oil
2 cloves garlic,
   chopped
2 teaspoons chopped
   marjoram
2 tablespoons
   chopped parsley
1½ tablespoons
   capers, chopped
salt and pepper
1 tablespoon lemon
   juice
GARNISH:
sautéed potatoes
lemon wedges

Place the chops side by side in a glass dish, spoon the oil over them and sprinkle with the garlic. Cover and marinate for 2 hours, turning once.

Strain the marinade into a large skillet, add the herbs and capers and heat gently. Add the chops and sauté for 5 minutes on each side. Season with salt and pepper to taste, sprinkle with the lemon juice and cook, covered, over low heat for 5 minutes.

Spoon the potatoes onto a warmed serving platter and arrange the chops around the edge. Spoon some of the pan juices over the chops and garnish with lemon wedges.
Serves 4

Animelle con Piselli
Sweetbreads with Peas

1 lb sweetbreads
1 tablespoon vinegar
2 tablespoons oil
3 tablespoons butter
1 teaspoon chopped
  sage
6 tablespoons
  Marsala
1 teaspoon lemon
  juice
salt and pepper
1 pkg (10 oz) frozen
  peas, cooked and
  drained
4 slices bacon, cooked
  and crumbled

Soak the sweetbreads in cold water
for 1 hour. Drain, cover with fresh
water and add the vinegar. Bring to a
boil and simmer for 5 minutes.

Drain and peel any membranes
from the sweetbreads, then cut into
1 inch pieces.

Heat the oil and butter in a skillet,
add the sage and sweetbreads and
cook over moderate heat, stirring
frequently, for 5 minutes. Add half
the Marsala and cook for about 5
minutes or until almost evaporated.

Add the remaining Marsala, the
lemon juice and salt and pepper to
taste. Simmer until reduced and
thickened. Stir in the peas and bacon
and serve immediately, with
noodles.
Serves 4

Rognoncini Trifolati

Sautéed Kidneys

1¼ lb veal or lamb
   kidneys
2 tablespoons vinegar
2 tablespoons oil
2 tablespoons butter
2 cloves garlic, finely
   chopped
2 tablespoons
   chopped parsley
1 tablespoon lemon
   juice
salt and pepper
toast triangles for
   garnish

Cover the kidneys with cold water, add the vinegar and soak for at least 30 minutes. Drain, cut out the core and thinly slice the kidneys.

Heat the oil and butter in a large skillet. Add the garlic and kidneys and sauté, stirring constantly, for 2 minutes. Add the parsley, lemon juice and salt and pepper to taste. Cook, stirring, for 1 to 2 minutes or until the kidneys are tender but juicy.

Serve immediately, garnished with toast triangles.

Serves 4

Polpette alla Siciliana

Meat Balls in Tomato Sauce

2 slices bread, crusts
   removed, soaked
   in milk and
   squeezed dry
1 lb lean ground beef
   or veal
2 cloves garlic,
   crushed
1 tablespoon chopped
   parsley
1 teaspoon finely
   grated lemon rind
¼ cup grated
   Parmesan cheese
grated nutmeg
salt and pepper
2 eggs, beaten
flour for coating
oil for frying
1¼ cups Salsa di
   Pomodori (see
   page 14)

Place the bread, meat, garlic, parsley, lemon rind, cheese, and nutmeg, salt and pepper to taste in a bowl. Add the eggs and mix together lightly but thoroughly. Gently shape the mixture into 1 inch balls. Roll lightly in flour, then chill in the refrigerator until ready to cook.

Pour the oil into a large skillet to a depth of ¼ inch and place over moderate heat. When hot, add the meat balls, a few at a time, and sauté for 3 to 4 minutes, turning, until brown on all sides. Lift out and drain on paper towels. Pour off the fat, leaving any residue in the pan.

Add the *Salsa di pomodori* (tomato sauce) to the skillet and thin to a pouring consistency with water if necessary. Return the meat balls to the pan, stir gently and simmer for 15 to 20 minutes or until cooked through.

Serves 4

Pollo con Rosmarino
Chicken with Rosemary

1 2½-3 lb
   broiler/fryer, cut
   up
salt and pepper
¼ cup oil
4 tablespoons butter
2-3 rosemary sprigs
2-3 cloves garlic
½ cup dry white
   wine or chicken
   stock

Season the chicken with salt and pepper. Heat the oil, butter, rosemary and garlic in a large skillet. Add the chicken and cook for 10 to 12 minutes or until golden, turning once.

Add the wine or stock and bring to just below boiling point. Simmer, uncovered, for 20 to 30 minutes or until tender. Place the chicken on a warmed serving platter and keep hot.

Remove the rosemary and garlic and spoon off the surplus fat from the skillet. Add 2 to 4 tablespoons water to the pan juices and bring to a boil, stirring to incorporate the sediment. Pour over the chicken and serve.
Serves 4

Petti di Pollo al Limone

Chicken Breasts with Lemon

4 boned chicken
  breasts
flour for coating
salt and pepper
1 tablespoon oil
5 tablespoons butter
2 tablespoons lemon
  juice
3 tablespoons chicken
  stock or broth
3 tablespoons
  chopped parsley
lemon slices for
  garnish

Cut each chicken breast horizontally into two slices. Season the flour with salt and pepper and use to coat the chicken slices.

Heat the oil and 3 tablespoons of the butter in a large skillet, add the chicken and sauté for 5 to 6 minutes on each side or until tender. Place on a warmed serving platter and keep hot.

Add the lemon juice and stock to the pan juices, bring to a boil, stirring, and boil for 1 minute. Add the parsley and remaining butter and stir until blended.

Pour over the chicken and garnish with lemon slices to serve.

Serves 4

Pollo con Peperoni
Chicken with Peppers

flour for coating
salt and pepper
1 2½-3 lb broiler/fryer, cut up
3 tablespoons oil
1 onion, thinly sliced
1 clove garlic, crushed
¼ cup dry white vermouth
1 teaspoon chopped marjoram
1 can (8 oz) tomatoes
1 teaspoon sugar
1 large green pepper, seeded and sliced

Season the flour with salt and pepper and use to coat the chicken. Heat the oil in a large skillet, add the onion and chicken and sauté for 10 minutes or until golden. Pour off surplus oil.

Add the garlic, vermouth and marjoram to the skillet and simmer until the wine has almost completely evaporated. Add the tomatoes with their juice, the sugar and green pepper. Cover and simmer for 30 minutes or until the chicken is cooked. Lift the chicken onto a warmed serving platter and keep hot.

Boil the sauce briskly, uncovered, until reduced and thickened. Check the seasoning and spoon over the chicken to serve.
Serves 4

Pollo con Salsa d'Uovo
Chicken in Egg and Lemon Sauce

1 2½-3 lb broiler/fryer, cut up
salt and pepper
2 tablespoons oil
2 tablespoons butter
¼ cup all-purpose flour
1¼ cups chicken stock or broth
1 bay leaf
1 small marjoram sprig
2 egg yolks
1 tablespoon lemon juice
GARNISH:
1 tablespoon chopped parsley
lemon slices

Season the chicken with salt and pepper. Heat the oil and butter in a skillet, add the chicken and sauté for about 12 minutes or until golden. Remove and set aside. Pour off all but 2 tablespoons of the fat.

Add the flour to the skillet and cook, stirring, for 1 minute. Add the stock and bring to a boil, stirring. Return the chicken to the skillet and add the herbs. Cover and simmer for 30 minutes or until tender.

Place the chicken on a warmed serving platter. Discard the herbs. Blend the egg yolks and lemon juice with 3 tablespoons of the sauce. Add to the skillet and heat gently, stirring, until thickened; do not boil. Check seasoning and pour over the chicken. Garnish with parsley and lemon.
Serves 4

Pollo in Porchetta
Chicken with Ham and Fennel

1 3½ lb roasting
  chicken
salt and pepper
½ lb cooked ham,
  cut into thick strips
2 tablespoons
  chopped fennel
  stalks and leaves
2 cloves garlic,
  crushed
3 tablespoons butter,
  softened
lemon juice
GARNISH:
Finocchio Toscano
  (see page 72)
fennel leaves

Season the chicken inside and out
with salt and pepper. Mix together
the ham, fennel and garlic and use to
stuff the chicken. Rub all over with
the butter and place in a roasting
pan.

Cover and cook in a preheated
375°F oven for 1 hour. Uncover and
continue cooking, basting
frequently, for 30 to 45 minutes or
until tender and golden brown. Place
on a warmed serving platter and
keep hot.

Season the juices with salt, pepper
and lemon juice to taste and reheat.
Garnish the chicken with *Finocchio
alla toscano* (broiled fennel) and fennel
leaves. Pass the sauce separately.
Serves 4

64

Pollo alla Diavolo
Tuscan Broiled Chicken

1 2½-3 lb
  broiler/fryer, split
salt and pepper
MARINADE:
3 tablespoons olive
  oil
2 tablespoons lemon
  juice
2 cloves garlic,
  crushed
6 sage leaves
  (optional)

Skewer each wing and leg together.
Season liberally with salt and pepper.
  Mix the marinade ingredients
together in a shallow glass dish. Add
the chicken halves, turning to coat,
cover and chill for 4 hours, turning
once.
  Place the chicken, skin side down,
in the broiler. Cook 5 to 6 inches
from the source of heat for 12
minutes. Turn and cook for 12
minutes longer or until tender. Baste
frequently with the marinade while
broiling.
  Place on a warmed serving platter
and pour the pan juices over. Serve
with a green salad and crusty bread.
Serves 4

Filetti di Tacchino al Marsala

Turkey Breast with Marsala

flour for coating
salt and pepper
4 turkey cutlets
1 tablespoon oil
5 tablespoons butter
1 cup thinly sliced
  mushrooms
1 teaspoon lemon
  juice
2 tablespoons grated
  Parmesan cheese
6 tablespoons
  Marsala
2 tablespoons chicken
  stock or broth
cooked broccoli spears
  for garnish

Season the flour with salt and pepper and use to coat the turkey. Heat the oil and 3 tablespoons of the butter in a large skillet, add the turkey and sauté for 4 to 5 minutes on each side or until tender. Place on a warmed serving platter and keep hot.

Melt the remaining butter in the skillet, add the mushrooms and sauté for 3 minutes. Add the lemon juice and a little salt and spread over the turkey cutlets. Sprinkle with the Parmesan cheese.

Add the Marsala and stock to the skillet and boil rapidly, stirring, until reduced by half. Spoon over the turkey. Garnish with broccoli to serve.

Serves 4

NOTE: Chicken cutlets may be used instead of turkey if they are easier to obtain.

Filetti di Tacchino alla Valdostano

Turkey Breast with Ham and Cheese

flour for coating
salt and pepper
4 turkey cutlets
1 egg, beaten
2 tablespoons oil
2 tablespoons butter
4 slices cooked ham
4 slices Bel Paese or
   Mozzarella cheese
parsley sprigs for
   garnish

Season the flour with salt and pepper and use to coat the turkey, then dip into the egg to coat. Heat the oil and butter in a large skillet, add the turkey and sauté for about 4 minutes on each side. Drain and transfer to the broiler.

Cover each cutlet with a slice of ham and then with cheese. Broil for 1 minute or until the cheese is golden and bubbling. Serve immediately, garnished with parsley.

Serves 4

NOTE: Chicken cutlets may be used instead of turkey.

Gallina alla Marsala
Cornish Hens in Marsala

4 cornish hens, about
   1 lb each
¼ cup olive oil
2 tablespoons butter
6 sage leaves,
   chopped
salt and pepper
1¼ cups Marsala
juice of 1 small
   lemon
½ cup pitted green
   olives
sage leaves for
   garnish

Wash the hens under cold running water and pat dry with paper towels. Heat the oil and butter in a large flameproof casserole or Dutch oven. Add the hens and brown on all sides. Remove the casserole from the heat and add the sage with salt and pepper to taste. Pour in the Marsala.

Cover and bake in a preheated 350°F oven for 50 minutes to 1 hour, basting several times with the pan juices, and adding more Marsala if necessary. Remove the hens to a warmed serving platter.

Skim off excess fat from the cooking liquid. Place the casserole over medium heat and stir in the lemon juice and olives. Cook until just heated through, then pour the sauce over the hens. Serve immediately, garnished with sage.
Serves 6

Pollo alla Cacciatora
Chicken Cacciatora

1 3-3½ lb
   broiler/fryer, cut
   up
salt and pepper
¼ cup olive oil
1 onion, chopped
½ lb mushrooms,
   sliced
2 cloves garlic,
   crushed
1 tablespoon chopped
   basil
1 can (16 oz)
   tomatoes, chopped
½ cup dry white
   wine
2 tablespoons
   chopped parsley

Season the chicken well with salt and pepper. Heat the oil in a large skillet, add the chicken and brown well on all sides. Remove the chicken and set aside.

Add the onion, mushrooms and garlic to the skillet and cook until softened. Add the basil, tomatoes and wine and stir well. Bring to a boil, then lower the heat and add the chicken. Cover and cook for 25 minutes or until chicken is tender.

Remove the chicken to a warmed serving platter. Bring the sauce to a boil and boil vigorously until slightly reduced and thickened. Spoon the sauce over the chicken and garnish with chopped parsley.
Serves 4

Anitra alla Venezia
Venetian Roast Duck

1 5 lb duck
salt and pepper
2 teaspoons chopped
 sage
2 stalks celery,
 chopped
1 small onion,
 chopped
1 clove garlic,
 chopped
¼ cup Marsala
juice of 1 orange
⅔ cup chicken stock
 or broth
1 teaspoon lemon
 juice
GARNISH:
orange slices
parsley sprigs

Season the duck cavity liberally with salt and pepper and insert the sage, celery, onion and garlic. Prick the skin all over and place the duck, breast side down, on a rack in a roasting pan.

Cook in a preheated 350°F oven for 1½ hours. Drain off the fat from the pan and turn the duck over. Heat the Marsala and orange juice and pour over the duck.

Continue roasting for 1 hour, or until tender, basting occasionally.

Place the duck on a warmed serving platter and keep hot. Skim the fat from the pan juices, add the stock and lemon juice and bring to a boil. Check the seasoning and strain into a sauceboat.

Garnish the duck with orange slices and parsley to serve.
Serves 4

Coniglio en Padella
Rabbit Stewed with Vegetables

1 eggplant, cut into 1
   inch cubes
salt and pepper
3 tablespoons olive
   oil
1 stalk celery,
   chopped
1 2-2½ lb rabbit, cut
   up
2 slices bacon, cooked
   and crumbled
4 large tomatoes,
   peeled and
   chopped
1 clove garlic,
   chopped
2 teaspoons chopped
   marjoram
2 teaspoons chopped
   parsley
¼ cup Marsala
1 cup chicken stock
   or broth
1 red or green
   pepper, seeded and
   thinly sliced

Place the eggplant in a colander,
sprinkle with salt and let stand for 1
hour.

Meanwhile, heat the oil in a large
skillet, add the celery and sauté for 2
minutes. Add the rabbit pieces and
cook until lightly browned. Add the
bacon, tomatoes, garlic, herbs and a
little salt and pepper and cook,
stirring, for 1 to 2 minutes.

Add the Marsala, bring to a boil
and simmer for about 5 minutes or
until well reduced. Stir in the stock,
cover and simmer for 30 minutes.

Drain the eggplant and pat dry
with paper towels. Add to the skillet
with the sliced pepper and simmer
for 30 minutes or until the rabbit is
tender. Place the rabbit on a warmed
serving platter and keep hot.

If the sauce is too thin, boil briskly
for about 5 minutes or until well
reduced. Check the seasoning and
spoon over the rabbit.
Serves 4

Finocchio alla Toscano
Tuscan Broiled Fennel

1¼ lb fennel bulbs
salt and pepper
1 thick slice lemon
1 tablespoon oil
2 tablespoons butter
¼ cup grated
    Parmesan cheese
fennel leaves for
    garnish (optional)

Trim the fennel bulbs and remove any discolored skin with a potato peeler. Cut vertically into ¾ inch thick pieces. Place in a saucepan with a pinch of salt, the lemon and oil and add enough boiling water to cover. Cook for 20 minutes or until just tender. Drain well.

Melt the butter in a gratin pan or shallow flameproof casserole, add the fennel and turn to coat. Season to taste with pepper and sprinkle with the cheese.

Place under a preheated broiler and cook until lightly browned. Serve immediately, garnished with fennel leaves if desired.
Serves 4

Peperonata
Peppers with Tomatoes

¼ cup oil
1 large onion,
 chopped
2 cloves garlic,
 crushed
2 bay leaves
6 large green
 peppers, halved
 and seeded
1 lb tomatoes, peeled
 and chopped
salt and pepper

Heat the oil in a skillet, add the onion, garlic and bay leaves and sauté for 5 minutes, stirring occasionally.

Cut the peppers into ½ inch strips and add to the skillet. Stir lightly, then cover and cook over low heat for 10 minutes.

Add the tomatoes and a little salt and pepper and cook uncovered, stirring frequently, until most of the liquid has evaporated and the mixture is fairly thick. Remove the bay leaves and check the seasoning.

Serve hot with broiled chicken, chops or steaks, or cold as an antipasto.
Serves 4

Sformata di spinaci
Spinach Pudding

4 tablespoons butter
1 onion, grated
2 pkgs (10 oz each)
　frozen chopped
　spinach, thawed
¼ cup all-purpose
　flour
1 cup milk
¼ cup grated
　Parmesan cheese
3 eggs, separated
salt and pepper
grated nutmeg
1¼ cups Salsa di
　Pomodori (see
　page 14)

Melt half the butter in a saucepan, add the onion and sauté for 5 minutes. Stir in the spinach, cover and cook for 5 minutes. Uncover and cook, stirring, until all moisture has evaporated.

Melt the remaining butter in a clean saucepan, add the flour and cook, stirring, until browned. Add the milk and cook, stirring, for 2 minutes or until thick and smooth. Remove from the heat and beat in the cheese, egg yolks, spinach, and salt, pepper and nutmeg to taste.

Beat the egg whites until stiff and fold into the mixture. Spoon into a well buttered 1½ quart bowl and cover with buttered foil. Place in a deep roasting pan half-filled with boiling water. Cook in a preheated 350°F oven for about 1 hour or until firm in the center.

Let stand for 5 minutes, then invert onto a warmed serving platter and pour the sauce over.
Serves 4

Fagioli alla Toscana
White Beans with Tomatoes

2 cans (16 oz each)
    cannellini beans,
    drained (see
    below)
3 tablespoons olive
    oil
2 cloves garlic,
    crushed
½ teaspoon dried
    sage
1 can (8 oz)
    tomatoes, drained
    and chopped
salt and pepper

Rinse the beans with cold water and drain.

Heat the oil, garlic and sage together gently in a saucepan for 1 to 2 minutes, then stir in the beans.

Add the tomatoes with salt and pepper to taste and stir gently. Cover and simmer for 10 minutes.

Serve hot as a vegetable, or cold topped with tuna fish as an antipasto.
Serves 4

NOTE: If cannellini beans are unobtainable, cover 1 cup dried white beans with boiling water and soak overnight. Next day, simmer gently for 1½ to 2 hours or until tender, drain and use as above.

Zucchini Ripieni
Cheese-Stuffed Zucchini

6 medium-size
    zucchini, about 5
    inches long
salt and pepper
2 slices white bread,
    crusts removed,
    soaked in 2
    tablespoons milk
½ cup Ricotta cheese
1 clove garlic,
    crushed
¼ teaspoon dried
    oregano
⅓ cup grated
    Parmesan cheese
1 egg yolk

Par boil the zucchini in boiling salted water for 5 minutes; drain. Cut in half lengthwise and scoop out the centers; finely chop. Reserve the shells.

Squeeze the bread dry, reserving the liquid, and mix with the chopped zucchini and remaining ingredients; add a little of the reserved milk if necessary to give a spreading consistency. Add salt and pepper to taste.

Fill the zucchini shells with the mixture and arrange in a well oiled shallow baking dish.

Cook in a preheated 375°F oven, for 35 to 40 minutes or until tender and golden.
Serves 4

Funghi Ripieni
Stuffed Mushrooms

---

12 large mushrooms
5-6 tablespoons olive oil
1 large onion, chopped
1 clove garlic, crushed
1 cup soft bread crumbs
½ cup diced cooked ham
2 tablespoons chopped parsley
2 tablespoons grated Parmesan cheese
salt and pepper
parsley sprigs for garnish

Remove the stems from the mushrooms and finely chop. Heat 3 tablespoons of the oil in a skillet, add the onion, garlic and chopped mushroom stems and cook gently for 5 minutes. Add the bread crumbs and cook until crisp, then stir in the ham, parsley, cheese and salt and pepper to taste.

Arrange the mushroom caps, hollow side up, in a greased shallow baking dish. Fill with the stuffing and sprinkle with a little oil.

Cover loosely with foil. Bake in a preheated 375°F oven for 25 minutes.

Serve hot, garnished with parsley, as an appetizer, or with chicken, meat or fish.

Serves 4

Gnocchi di Patate
Potato Gnocchi

1½ cups all-purpose flour, sifted
1 egg, beaten
salt and pepper
grated nutmeg
1 lb potatoes, cooked and mashed
TO SERVE:
2 tablespoons butter
¼ cup grated Parmesan cheese
Salsa di Fegatini or Salsa di Carne (see pages 12-13)

Combine the flour, egg, and salt, pepper and nutmeg to taste with the potatoes. Mix well to form a firm dough. With floured hands, shape pieces of the dough into long rolls, about ½ inch thick. Cut into ¾ inch lengths and curve by denting with a little finger.

Cook in batches, by dropping into a large pot of boiling salted water and simmering for 3 to 5 minutes or until they rise to the surface. Lift out with a slotted spoon and drain. Place in a buttered shallow baking dish, dot with the butter and sprinkle with the Parmesan.

Bake in a preheated 400°F oven for 7 to 10 minutes.

Divide between individual dishes and pour the sauce over.

Serves 4

Melanzane alla Parmigiana
Eggplant and Tomato Pie

1 eggplant, about
   1½ lb
salt and pepper
flour for coating
6 tablespoons olive
   oil
   (approximately)
1¼ cups Salsa di
   Pomodori (see
   page 14)
¼ lb Mozzarella or
   Bel Paese cheese,
   thinly sliced
3 tablespoons grated
   Parmesan cheese

Cut the eggplant lengthwise into
¼ inch slices. Sprinkle with salt,
place in a colander and let stand for 1
hour. Pat dry with paper towels,
then coat lightly with flour.

Heat half the oil in a large skillet,
add half the eggplant slices and sauté
until lightly browned on both sides.
Remove with a slotted spoon and
drain on paper towels. Repeat with
the remaining oil and eggplant slices.

Arrange alternate layers of
eggplant, *Salsa di pomodori* (tomato
sauce) and Mozzarella in a greased
1½ quart casserole, sprinkling each
layer with pepper and Parmesan and
finishing with Parmesan.

Bake in a preheated 400°F oven for
25 to 30 minutes or until golden.
Serves 4

Insalata Mista
Italian Mixed Salad

Raw young spinach leaves are widely used for salads in Italy – when available, they make a nice change from lettuce. For a really crisp salad, after washing and thoroughly drying the lettuce or spinach, place in a plastic bag and chill in the refrigerator for a few hours.

1 head lettuce, or
   ¼ lb young
   spinach leaves
½ green pepper,
   seeded and sliced
2 tomatoes, sliced
½ cucumber, sliced
6 radishes, sliced
DRESSING:
3 tablespoons olive
   oil
1 tablespoon lemon
   juice
1 clove garlic,
   crushed
salt and pepper

Tear the lettuce or spinach leaves into pieces. Place in a salad bowl and top with the remaining vegetables.

Put the dressing ingredients in a screw-top jar, adding salt and pepper to taste, and shake well.

Sprinkle the dressing over the salad and toss lightly. Serve immediately.

Serves 4

Insalata di Finocchio
Fennel Salad

1 large fennel bulb
½ greenhouse
   cucumber, diced
4 radishes, sliced
2 oranges, divided
   into segments
DRESSING:
2 tablespoons olive
   oil
2 teaspoons lemon
   juice
1 clove garlic,
   crushed
2 teaspoons chopped
   mint
salt and pepper

Trim the stalks, base and coarse outer leaves from the fennel. Cut lengthwise into thin slices, then into strips.

Place in a salad bowl with the cucumber, radishes and orange segments.

Put the dressing ingredients in a screw-top jar, adding salt and pepper to taste, and shake well. Sprinkle over the vegetables and toss lightly. Serve immediately.

Serves 4

Insalata di Rinforza
Cauliflower Salad

1 cauliflower, broken
into florets
salt and pepper
5 tablespoons olive
oil
1½ tablespoons red
wine vinegar
1 tablespoon capers
1 tablespoon chopped
parsley
few ripe olives
1 can (2 oz) anchovy
fillets, drained and
sliced

Cook the cauliflower in boiling
salted water for 5 to 6 minutes or
until cooked but firm. Drain and
rinse under cold running water.

Mix the oil, vinegar and a little salt
and pepper together in a salad bowl.
Add the cauliflower and toss gently.
Sprinkle with the capers, parsley and
olives. Arrange the anchovy fillets in
a lattice pattern on top. Serve
immediately.

Serves 4

Insalata di Riso
Rice Salad

1⅓ cups water
½ teaspoon salt
1⅓ cups pre-cooked
 rice
¼ cup olive oil
1 tablespoon wine
 vinegar
2 scallions, finely
 chopped
1 small green pepper,
 seeded and thinly
 sliced
salt and pepper
¼ greenhouse
 cucumber, diced
2 tablespoons
 chopped parsley
lettuce leaves to
 serve

Bring the water and salt to a boil in a saucepan. Add the rice, stir well, cover and remove from the heat. Let stand for 10 minutes or until the liquid is absorbed. Fluff the rice with a fork.

Combine the oil, vinegar, scallions, green pepper and salt and pepper to taste in a bowl. Add the hot rice and thoroughly toss. Cover and let stand until cold.

Just before serving, stir in the cucumber and parsley. Line a shallow bowl with lettuce, spoon the rice salad into the center and serve immediately.

Serves 4 to 6

DESSERTS

Melone con Fragoline
Melon with Strawberries

1 melon
confectioners sugar
1 pint strawberries
2 tablespoons
   Cointreau or
   Grand Marnier
juice of ½ lemon

Cut a 'lid' off the top of the melon and reserve. Scoop out the fruit with a melon baller, discarding the seeds. Reserve the shell. Sprinkle the melon balls with a little confectioners sugar, cover and chill until required. Sprinkle the strawberries with the liqueur, lemon juice and confectioners sugar to taste, cover and chill until required.

Just before serving, mix the melon and strawberries together, spoon into the melon shell and cover with the 'lid'. Serve on a bed of crushed ice decorated with flowers and mint if desired.

Serves 4

Pesche alla Piemontese
Stuffed Peaches

4 large firm peaches,
   halved and pitted
¾ cup macaroon or
   amaretti cookie
   crumbs
¼ cup sugar
3 tablespoons butter,
   softened
1 egg yolk
½ teaspoon finely
   grated lemon rind
sliced almonds to
   decorate (optional)

Scoop a little fruit from the center of each peach half and place in a bowl. Add the crumbs, sugar, 2 tablespoons of the butter, the egg yolk and lemon rind and beat until smooth.

Divide between the peaches, shaping the stuffing into a mound. Sprinkle with almonds, if desired, and dot with the remaining butter. Arrange in a buttered baking dish.

Bake in a preheated 350°F oven for 25 to 35 minutes. Serve warm or cold with cream.

Serves 4

Zabaglione

4 egg yolks
¼ cup sugar
½ cup Marsala
lady fingers to serve

Put the egg yolks and sugar in the top of a double boiler, over boiling water, and beat until pale and fluffy, making sure the water does not touch the bottom of the double boiler. Beat in the Marsala. Continue beating until the mixture begins to thicken and doubles in volume. Spoon into wine glasses and serve immediately, with lady fingers.
Serves 4

Cassata alla Siciliana

3 eggs
½ cup sugar
½ teaspoon finely
  grated lemon rind
1 teaspoon vanilla
¾ cup all-purpose
  flour, sifted
FILLING AND
  FROSTING:
2 cups ricotta cheese
½ cup sugar
¼ cup Cointreau
2 squares (1 oz each)
  semi-sweet
  chocolate, finely
  chopped
¼ cup diced mixed
  candied fruit
1 tablespoon chopped
  almonds or
  pistachio nuts
TO DECORATE:
glacé cherries
crystallized orange
  and lemon slices
chocolate curls

Beat the eggs, sugar, lemon rind and vanilla together until thick and fluffy. Fold in the flour.

Pour into a greased 8 × 4 inch loaf pan. Bake in a preheated 375°F oven for 25 minutes or until a toothpick inserted in the center comes out clean. Invert onto a wire rack to cool.

Beat the cheese and sugar together until smooth. Add 2 tablespoons of the Cointreau. Divide the mixture in half. Place one portion in the refrigerator; add the chocolate, candied fruit and nuts to the other portion for the filling.

Cut the cake horizontally into three layers. Place the bottom layer on a serving platter and sprinkle with 1 tablespoon Cointreau. Spread with half the filling, cover with another cake layer and sprinkle with the remaining Cointreau. Spread the remaining filling over and top with the last cake layer. Gently press the cake together and refrigerate.

One hour before serving, remove cake and reserved frosting mixture from the refrigerator. Spread frosting over top and sides of the gâteau. Decorate with cherries, orange and lemon slices and chocolate curls.
Serves 6 to 8

Crostata Dolce di Ricotta

Italian Cheese Pie

PASTRY:
*2 cups all-purpose
flour, sifted*
1/3 cup sugar
*1/2 cup butter,
softened*
*1 teaspoon finely
grated lemon rind*
2 egg yolks

FILLING:
*1 1/2 cups Ricotta
. cheese*
1/3 cup sugar
3 eggs, beaten
*1 teaspoon grated
lemon rind*
*1 teaspoon grated
orange rind*
*1/2 cup diced mixed
candied fruit*
*1/4 cup chopped
almonds*
*confectioners sugar
for sprinkling*

Sift the flour and sugar into a bowl, make a well in the center and add the butter, lemon rind and egg yolks. Gradually draw the flour into the center, using your fingertips, and work the ingredients to a firm, smooth dough. Cover and chill for 1 hour.

Meanwhile, prepare the filling. Mix the cheese and sugar together in a bowl. Gradually beat in the eggs, then add the remaining ingredients. Mix well.

Roll out the dough and use to line an 8 inch flan or quiche pan. Spread the filling evenly in the pastry shell.

Bake in a preheated 350°F oven for 45 to 50 minutes. Cool slightly, then remove to a wire rack and let stand until cold. Sprinkle the pie with confectioners sugar just before serving.

Serves 6 to 8

NOTE: If preferred, decorate the pie with a lattice pattern of pastry strips, before baking.

Nocciollette
Hazelnut Cookies

¾ *cup hazelnuts*
½ *cup butter*
6 *tablespoons*
  confectioners sugar
1½ *tablespoons*
  honey
1 *cup all-purpose*
  flour, sifted
confectioners sugar
  for dusting

Spread the nuts on a cookie sheet and toast under a preheated broiler, shaking frequently until the skins split. Place the nuts in a towel and rub off the loose skins. Coarsely grind.

Cream the butter, sugar and honey together until fluffy. Add the flour and nuts and mix to a dough.

With lightly floured hands, shape teaspoonfuls of the dough into ovals and place about 2 inches apart on lightly greased cookie sheets.

Bake in a preheated 350°F oven for about 15 minutes or until firm. Cool slightly, then roll in confectioners sugar. Place on a wire rack and let stand until cooled. Store in an airtight container.
Makes about 24

Pastini di Mandorle

Almond and Apricot Cookies

½ cup butter,
softened
1 cup sugar
1 egg, beaten
⅛ teaspoon almond
extract
2 cups all-purpose
flour
1 teaspoon baking
powder
1 tablespoon milk
(approximately)
½ cup finely
chopped almonds
2 tablespoons apricot
jam

Cream the butter and sugar together until light and fluffy, then beat in the egg and almond extract. Sift the flour and baking powder together and stir into the mixture with enough milk to make a smooth paste.

Roll teaspoonfuls of the mixture into balls. Roll in chopped almonds and place well apart on a greased cookie sheet. Make a deep dent in the center of each and fill with jam.

Bake in a preheated 400°F oven for 12 to 15 minutes or until golden. Let stand for 5 minutes, then remove to a wire rack and leave until cooled. Store in an airtight container.
Makes about 36

Gelato alla Nocciola

Hazelnut Ice Cream

1 cup hazelnuts,
toasted and
skinned (see
Nocciollette, page
87)
1¼ cups milk
4 egg yolks
½ cup sugar
⅛ teaspoon vanilla
¾ cup heavy cream,
whipped

Reserve a few nuts for decoration if desired; coarsely grind the remainder.

Place the milk in a saucepan and bring to a boil. Cream together the egg yolks, sugar and vanilla in a bowl until pale, then gradually stir in the milk. Stir in the ground nuts.

Pour into a clean saucepan and heat gently, stirring, until the mixture is thick enough to coat the back of the spoon; do not allow to boil. Cover and let stand until cold, stirring occasionally.

Fold in the whipped cream. Spoon into a freezerproof container, cover and freeze until firm.

Place in the refrigerator 20 minutes before serving to soften. Decorate with reserved nuts, if desired.
Serves 4 to 5

Gelato di Fragole
Strawberry Ice Cream

1 pint strawberries
juice of ½ orange
2 teaspoons lemon
 juice
¾ cup confectioners
 sugar
1 cup heavy cream
few strawberries,
 halved, to decorate

Process the strawberries in a blender or food processor, then strain. Stir in the orange and lemon juices and sweeten to taste with confectioners sugar. Whip the cream until thick but not stiff. Gently fold in the strawberry mixture. Pour into a freezerproof container, cover and freeze until firm.

Place in the refrigerator 20 minutes before serving to soften. Spoon into individual glass dishes and decorate with strawberries.

Serves 4

Granita di Arancia
Orange Water Ice

1 cup sugar
2½ cups water
1¼ cups orange juice
2 tablespoons lemon
  juice
1 teaspoon finely
  grated orange rind

Place the sugar and water in a
saucepan over moderate heat and stir
until dissolved. Bring to a boil and
boil for 5 minutes. Cool to room
temperature, then stir in the fruit
juices and orange rind.

Pour into an ice cube tray. Freeze
until mushy stirring every 30
minutes.

Spoon into four tall glasses and
serve immediately, with a straw or
spoon.

Serves 4

NOTE: If the ice freezes solid, remove
to the refrigerator to soften until it
can be mashed with a fork.

Granita di Limone
Prepare as above, replacing the
orange and lemon juice and orange
rind with 1¼ cups fresh lemon juice.

Gelato Agli Amaretti

Amaretti Ice Cream Bombe

1 cup amaretti
   cookies
3 tablespoons
   Marsala or dry
   sherry
   (approximately)
2 cups vanilla ice
   cream (see below)
TO DECORATE:
whipped cream
   (optional)
amaretti cookies

Grind the amaretti in a blender or food processor or crush with a rolling pin. Mix with the Marsala to form a soft paste.

Spread two-thirds of the ice cream over the bottom and up the sides of a 3 cup bowl. Spread the amaretti mixture in the center and cover with the remaining ice cream, smoothing the top. Cover with foil and freeze until firm.

Invert the bombe onto a serving plate and place in the refrigerator 30 minutes before serving to soften. Decorate with whipped cream and amaretti cookies, if desired.

Serves 4

NOTE: Avoid soft ice cream otherwise the bombe will not hold its shape.

Panforte di Siena

This flat 'cake' with a nougat-like texture, rich with candied fruit, toasted nuts and spices, is a particular specialty of the town of Siena. Although it can be served as a dessert to complete a light meal, Italians would be more likely to serve it with coffee in the morning or mid-afternoon.

¾ *cup hazelnuts*
¾ *cup chopped almonds*
1 *cup chopped mixed candied fruit*
¼ *cup unsweetened cocoa*
½ *cup all-purpose flour, sifted*
½ *teaspoon ground cinnamon*
¼ *teaspoon apple pie spice*
½ *cup sugar*
⅓ *cup honey*
TO FINISH:
2 *tablespoons confectioners sugar*
1 *teaspoon ground cinnamon*

Spread the hazelnuts on a cookie sheet and toast under the broiler, shaking frequently until the skins split. Place in a towel and rub off the loose skins. Coarsely grind the hazelnuts.

Place the hazelnuts, almonds, candied fruit, cocoa, flour and spices in a mixing bowl and stir well.

Put the sugar and honey in a saucepan and heat gently until the sugar has dissolved. Boil gently until a little of the mixture forms a soft ball when dropped into a cup of cold water. Remove from the heat and stir in the dry ingredients.

Press into a lined and greased 8 inch loose-bottom cake pan so that the mixture is no more than ¼ inch thick. Bake in a preheated 300°F oven for 30 to 35 minutes.

Remove from the pan and allow to cool. Peel off the lining paper and place on a serving platter. Mix the confectioners sugar with the cinnamon and sift over the 'cake'. Serve cut into wedges.
Serves 8 to 10

INDEX